DUMB

GW00400236

DUMBER

★★★★★★★★★

The Joe Biden & Kamala Harris Book of Stupid Quotes

Copyright © 2022 by Owen Monie
All rights reserved. This book or any portion thereof may
not be reproduced or used in any manner whatsoever
without the express written permission of the publisher
except for the use of brief quotations in a book review.

Printed in the United States of America

INTRODUCTION

"Biden's an empty vessel. I don't think he has any firm principles."

Noam Chomsky
American linguist
and cognitive scientist

"I think he has been wrong on nearly every major foreign policy and national security issue over the past four decades."

Robert Gates
Former U.S. Defense Secretary

"Don't underestimate Joe's ability to f**k things up."

President Barack Obama

"Let's be clear, Kamala Harris may be the dumbest person ever elected vice president in American history."

Newt Gingrich
Former Speaker of the House

"Every time she speaks, it's like watching Wile E. Coyote's feet keep spinning madly even after he's run off the cliff."

Kyle Smith
American critic and columnist

THE QUOTES

"Let me start off with two words: Made in America."

"I've been sleeping with a teacher for a long time. But it's always been the same teacher."

"I am Kamala Harris, my pronouns are she and her, and I am a woman sitting at the table wearing a blue suit."

"Representative Jackie — are you here? Where's Jackie?"

Biden looking for Indiana Rep. Jackie Walorski at a White House conference — eight weeks after her death.

"When we talk about the children of the community, they are a children of the community."

"You had to put on your windshield wipers to get, literally, the oil slick off the window. That's why I and so damn many other people I grew up with have cancer."

"If we do everything right, if we do it with absolute certainty, there's still a 30 percent chance we're going to get it wrong."

"It is time for us to do what we have been doing and that time is every day."

"You're full of sh*t. Don't try me, pal. Do you want to go outside? I'm not working. Give me a break, man, don't be such a horse's a**."

Biden to Detroit factor worker.

"We've got to take this stuff seriously, as seriously as you are because you have been forced to take this seriously."

"Folks, I can tell you I've known eight presidents, three of them intimately."

"We'll always honor the bravery and selfishness — selflessness of the — and sacrifices of the Americans who served."

"What else do we know about this population, 18 through 24? They are stupid!"

"And continue to bear witness, to keep alive the truth and honor of the Holocaust."

"Of course people have to prove who they are, but not in a way that makes it almost impossible for them to prove who they are."

"There have not been many senators from Delaware. It's a small state. As a matter of fact, there has never been one."

"A man I'm proud to call my friend. A man who will be the next President of the United States – Barack America!"

At his first U.S. presidential campaign rally with Barack Obama.

"And I haven't been to Europe.
And I mean, I don't understand the point that you're making."

In response to a question whether she had personally visited the United States-Mexico border.

"I'm also sending to Congress a comprehensive package of that will enhance our underlying effort to accommodate the Russian oligarchs and make sure we take their take their, their ill-begotten gains. Ha, we're going to 'accommodate' them. We're going to seize their yachts, their luxury homes, and other ill-begotten gains of Putin's kleptocrac-yeah, kleptocracy and klep- the guys who are the kleptocracies. But these are bad guys."

"For God's sake, this man cannot remain in power. Putin may circle Kyiv with tanks, but he will never gain the hearts and souls of the Iranian people."

"Never let anybody suggest to you that you are what they think you should be, you tell them who you are and who you know you are, and what you intend to be. Got that?"

"And, by the way, the 20, the 200 mil- the 200,000 people that have died on his watch, how many of those have survived?"

Reporter: Do you think inflation is a political liability in the midterms?

Biden: No, it's a great asset — more inflation. What a stupid son of a b**ch.

"The next Republican that tells me I'm not religious, I'm gonna shove my rosary beads down their throat!"

"And within the context then of the fact that that window is still opening, although open, although it is absolutely narrowing, but within the context of a diplomatic path still being open, the deterrence effect, we believe, has merit."

"And Corn Pop was a bad dude. And he ran a bunch of bad boys. And back in those days—to show how things have changed—one of the things you had to use, if you used Pomade in your hair, you had to wear a baby cap. And so he was up on the board and wouldn't listen to me. I said, 'Hey, Esther, you! Off the board, or I'll come up and drag you off.' Well, he came off, and he said, 'I'll meet you outside.' My car was mostly, these were all public housing behind us, my car—there was a gate on here. I parked my car outside the gate. And he said, 'I'll be waiting for you.' He was waiting for me with three guys with straight razors. Not a joke."

"Thank you, Boris. And I want to thank, er ... that fella Down Under. Thank you very much, pal."

President Biden forgetting the name of Australian Prime Minister Scott Morrison.

"Ukraine is a country in Europe. It exists next to another country called Russia. Russia is a bigger country. Russia is a powerful country. Russia decided to invade a smaller country called Ukraine so basically that's wrong."

"In every single crisis we have had that I have been around, going back to Jimmy Carter and the hostages all the way through to this moment, presidents' ratings have always gone up in a crisis, but that old expression, the proof is going to be in eating the pudding."

"The United States shares a very important relationship, which is an alliance with the Republic of North Korea. And it is an alliance that is strong and enduring."

The longstanding U.S. ally is South Korea.

"Unless we do something about this, my children are going to grow up in a jungle, the jungle being a racial jungle with tensions having built so high that it is going to explode at some point."

Busing of schoolchildren hearing before the Committee on the Judiciary, 1977.

"And in those days, you remember the straight razors, you had to bang 'em on the curb, gettin' em rusty, puttin' em in the rain barrel, gettin' em rusty?"

"So to that end, we are announcing today also that we will assist Jamaica in COVID recovery by assisting in terms of the recovery efforts in Jamaica that have been essential to, I believe, what is necessary to strengthen not only the issue of public health but also the economy."

"I remember spending time at the, you know, going to the, you know, the Tree of Life synagogue, speaking with them."

Biden has never visited the Tree of Life synagogue.

Reporter: Why are you so confident that Russian President Vladimir Putin will change his behavior?

Biden: I'm not confident he'll change his behavior! What the hell? What do you do all of the time? When did I say I was confident?

"I think that, to be very honest with you, I — I do believe that we should have rightly believed, but we certainly believed that certain issues are just settled. Certain issues are just settled."

"I'd rather be at home making love to my wife while my children are asleep."

"Our world is more interconnected and interdependent. That is especially true when it comes to the climate crisis, which is why we will work together, and continue to work together, to address these issues, to tackle these challenges, and to work together as we continue to work operating from the new norms, rules, and agreements, that we will convene to work together on to galvanize global action. With that I thank you all. This is a matter of urgent priority for all of us and I know we will work on this together."

"You know, I'm embarrassed. Do you know the website number? I should have it in front of me and I don't.
I'm actually embarrassed."

"A successful dump!"

**Explaining his whereabouts
(dropping deadwood at the dump)
to the reporters outside his home.**

"I love Hanukkah because it really is about the light, and bringing light where there has been darkness. And there is so much work to be done in the world, to bring light."

"And I want to thank the sec — the, the, ah former general, I keep calling him general, but my, my — the guy who runs that outfit over there."

"If Haiti, a God-awful thing to say, if Haiti just quietly sunk into the Caribbean or rose up 300 feet, it wouldn't matter a whole lot in terms of our interest."

"I probably have a much higher IQ than you do, I suspect."

Biden's records indicate he graduated 76th out of a law school class of 85. His undergraduate academic records show that he graduated from Delaware 506th in a class of 688 with a "C" average.

"I love Venn diagrams, so... I just do! Whenever you're dealing with conflict, pull out a Venn diagram, right? You know, the three circles..."

"I am a gaffe machine. But by God, what a wonderful thing compared to a guy who can't tell the truth."

"In Delaware, the largest growth in population is Indian-Americans, moving from India. You cannot go to a 7-Eleven or a Dunkin' Donuts unless you have a slight Indian accent. And I'm not joking."

"Ain't that a b**ch?" I mean … excuse me, the vice president thing? I'm joking, I'm joking. Best decision I ever made."

To a Harvard University student who identified himself as the student body's vice president.

"When you see our kids, and I truly believe that they are our children, they are the children of our country, of our communities, I mean, our future is really bright if we prioritize them, and therefore prioritize the climate crisis."

"I mean, you've got the first sort of mainstream African American who is articulate and bright and clean."

Biden said of then-Sen. Barack Obama as both campaigned ahead of the 2008 primaries.

"This is a bunch of stuff."

"The border is secure."

"Now is the time to heed the timeless advice from Teddy Roosevelt: 'Speak softly and carry a big stick.' I promise you, the president has a big stick."

In a 2012 speech on foreign policy, praising President Obama's approach to diplomacy.

"Clap for that, you stupid bastards. Man, you are a dull bunch. Must be slow here, man."

Biden speaking with U.S. troops stationed at Al Dhafra Air Base.

"This sounds quaint, and so I'm reluctant to say it, but, you know, I didn't eat a grape until I was in my 20s, like, literally, had never had a grape. I remember the first time I had a grape, I went, 'Wow! This is quite tasty.' It was absolutely ingrained so deeply in me: Never cross a picket line."

"We've got to recognize that a kid wearing a hoodie may very well be the next poet laureate not a gangbanger."

"No one f**ks with a Biden."

"You're gonna literally see the craters on the moon with your own eyes! With your own eyes! I'm telling you, it is gonna be unbelievable."

Harris faking her enthusiasm to a group of child actors for a NASA YouTube video about space exploration.

"Poor kids are just as bright and just as talented as white kids."

"The number one job facing the middle class, and it happens to be, as Barack says, a three-letter word: jobs. J-O-B-S."

"You're a damn liar, man. And by the way, I'm not sedentary. Let's do push-ups together, man, let's run, let's do whatever you want to do. Let's take an IQ test, all right? Look, look, fat, look. Here's the deal."

Biden to a voter at event in New Hampton, Iowa.

"We the people —
that's how our
Constitution starts —
or the Declaration.
We the people.
It's who we are."

"We must together work together to see where we are, where we are going, where we are headed, and our vision for where we should be. But also see it as a moment to, together, address the challenges and to work on the opportunities."

"Ever been to a caucus? No, you haven't. You're a lying dog-faced pony soldier."

Biden to a college student in New Hampshire during a campaign event.

"Well I'm telling you, if you have a problem figuring out whether you're for me or Trump, then you ain't black."

"Elections matter. And when folks vote, they order what they want — and in this case they got what they asked for. I went off script a little bit."

"We hold these truths to be self-evident: all men and women are created, by the, you know the, you know the thing."

"You know, there's a uh, during World War II, uh, you know, where Roosevelt came up with a thing uh, that uh, you know, was totally different than a, than the, the, it's called, he called it the, you know, the World War II, he had the war – the War Production Board."

"When the stock market crashed, Franklin Roosevelt got on the television and didn't just talk about the princes of greed. He said, 'Look, here's what happened.'"

Herbert Hoover was president during the 1929 Wall Street Crash and television was introduced to the public at the 1939 World's Fair in New York.

"I am here, standing here on the northern flank, on the eastern flank, talking about what we have in terms of the eastern flank and our NATO allies, and what is at stake at this very moment, what is at stake this very moment are some of the guiding principles…"

"I may be Irish but I'm not stupid."

"He's going to let the big banks once again write their own rules – unchain Wall Street. They're gonna put y'all back in chains."

Talking about Republican candidate Mitt Romney's plans to unshackle Wall Street, during the 2012 campaign, to an audience that included many African Americans.

"So we invested an additional $12 billion into community banks, because we know community banks are in the community and understand the needs and desires of that community as well as the talent and capacity of community, and that access to capital should not be a barrier to innovation and creativity and what we know those small businesses are, which is part of the economic lifeblood of a community and, by extension, all of society."

"His mom lived in Long Island for 10 years or so, God rest her soul and— although, she's … wait, your mom's still, your mom's still alive—is your dad passed. God bless her soul! I gotta' get this straight!"

Mistakenly asking for God's blessing of Irish Prime Minister Brian Cowen's living mother during a White House celebration of St. Patrick's Day.

"Barack Obama ain't taking my shotguns, so don't buy that malarkey. I've got two, if he tries to fool with my Beretta, he's got a problem."

"I can only assume that you will enjoy educating your family about how the Coast Guard is, quote, 'the hard nucleus around the Navy forms in times of war'. You are a — why, you're a really dull class. I mean, come on, man, is the sun getting to you?"

The quote is, "The Coast Guard is that hard nucleus about which the Navy forms in time of war." Ronald Reagan delivered it perfectly while giving the Coast Guard commencement speech in 1988.

"There's no sound or fume.... So how do I know it's working? How would I know that?"

Harris trying to figure out how an electric car works.

"I have not bent the law, but I have let imagination take hold in some places where I think it's consistent with the spirit of the law. Is that the best way of saying that? Yes, I should stop."

"If I had intended to cheat, would I have been so stupid? I value my word above all else."

In a letter to Syracuse University College of Law pleading not to be dismissed. This was after he "used five pages from a published law review article without quotation or attribution," according to a faculty report.

"But we all watched the television coverage of just yesterday. That's on top of everything else that we know and don't know yet, based on what we've just been able to see. And because we've seen it or not doesn't mean it hasn't happened."

"Chuck Graham, state senator, is here. Stand up, Chuck, let 'em see you. Oh, God love you. What am I talking about?"

To wheelchair-bound Missouri state senator, Charles Graham.

"I've adopted the attitude of the great Negro — at the time, pitcher in the Negro Leagues — went on to become a great pitcher in the pros — in the Major League Baseball after Jackie Robinson. His name was Satchel Paige."

"With us in government. We campaign with thee plan! Uppercase T uppercase P — thee plan! And then the environment is such that we're expected to defend — thee plan!"

In a lab in Paris, Harris took on faux French accent as she emphasized "thee plan!"

"You know there's an old Irish saying, there's all kinds of old Irish sayings. My grandfather Finnegan, I think he made them up. But uh, it says, may the hinges of our friendship never go rusty. Well, with these two folks that you're about to meet if you haven't already, there's no doubt about them staying oiled and lubricated here, ladies and gentlemen. Now for you who are not full Irish in this room, lubricated has a different meaning for us all."

"Why don't you say something nice instead of being a smarta** all the time?"

To a manager of a frozen custard shop in Milwaukee in 2010 when he offered him a free dessert in exchange for a tax cut.

"I cannot believe that a French man visiting Kiev went back home and told his colleagues he discovered something and didn't say he discovered the most beautiful women in the world. That's my observation."

Speaking to Ukrainian President Viktor Yushchenko in 2009.

"The significance of the passage of time, right? The significance of the passage of time. So when you think about it, there is great significance to the passage of time."

"I wouldn't go anywhere in confined places now. When one person sneezes it goes all the way through the aircraft. That's me. I would not be, at this point, if they had another way of transportation, suggesting they ride the subway."

"I did not walk in the shoes of generations of students who walked these grounds. But I walked other grounds. Because I'm so damn old, I was there as well. You think I'm kidding, man. It seems like yesterday the first time I got arrested. Anyway —"

There is no record of Biden being arrested.

"I guess what I'm trying to say without boring you too long at breakfast—and you all look dull as hell, I might add. The dullest audience I have ever spoken to. Just sitting there, staring at me. Pretend you like me!"

Interviewer: Best rapper alive?

Harris: Tupac

Interviewer: He's not...

Harris: I know, I keep doing it! (cackle)

Who would I say? I mean there's so many, I mean, you know, it, I, there are some that I would not mention right now because they should stay in their lane.

Interviewer: I don't know what that means...

"Putin knows that when I am president of the United States, his days of tyranny and trying to intimidate the United States and those in Eastern Europe are over!"

"With all due respect, that's a bunch of malarkey."

Printed in Great Britain
by Amazon

14894721R00061